Let's Write Together

Let's Write Together: Write Place, Write Time
15-Day Writing Journal

Copyright © 2019 Tina M. Beatty

All rights reserved. No part of this e-book may be used or reproduced, stored in a retrieval system or transmitted in any way by any means, electronic, mechanical, photocopy, recording or otherwise without the prior permission of the author.

Scripture quotations, unless otherwise indicated, are taken from the Holy Bible, King James Version.

Cover: D&K Productions

ISBN 13: 978-1-970057-02-7
ISBN 10: 1-970057-02-5

Interior Designer:
Enger Lanier Taylor – In Due Season Publishing

In Due Season Publishing, LLC
www.indueseasonpublishing.com
indueseasonpublishing@gmail.com

Dr. Tina M. Beatty

Limits of Liability and Disclaimer of Warranty

The author and publisher shall not be liable for your misuse of this material. This book is strictly for informational and educational purposes. The purpose of this book is to educate and entertain. The author and/or publisher do not guarantee that anyone following these techniques, suggestions, tips, ideas, or strategies will become successful. The author and/or publisher shall have neither liability nor responsibility to anyone with respect to any loss or damage caused, or alleged to be caused, directly or indirectly by the information contained in this book.

Very important to note that the contents of this book are NOT a substitute for medical advice. Neither should this information be interpreted as offering medical guidelines. Always discuss your health issues and concerns with your health care provider before beginning a fast. Under no circumstance is the contents of this book suggesting discontinuing your mediation. Please seek guidance from your health care provider who will make such determination.

While the author has made every effort to provide accurate internet addresses at the time of publication, neither the publisher nor the author assumes any responsibility for errors or for changes that occur after publication. Further, the publisher does not have any control over and does not assume any responsibility for author or third-party websites or their content.

Views expressed in this book do not necessarily reflect the views of the publisher.

Printed in the United States of America

Let's Write Together

Dr. Tina M. Beatty

Table of Contents

Testimonials from the Webinar	5
Introduction	9
Discovering the Writer Within	12
Word Count Chart	17
Twelve Writing Tips	19
Outline For 15 Day Writing Journey	23
Days 1-15	24-35
10 Launching Tips to Prepare You	36
About the Author	39
Blank Pages	41-106

Let's Write Together

Testimonials from the Webinar

Kenneth Williams

I've had a book that I feel, has been trapped inside of me since my brother's life was taken over 40 years ago, and writing the book in this class gave me the push that I needed to get started, so when I write, I'm FREE!

Micah Azariah

Throughout this whole process, God taught me never to stop dreaming, even when I feel as if a certain dream has died; that God can resurrect anything in His timing! When I was in college, I was a journalism major, I've always dreamt of being a writer but life got in the way and I couldn't finish school. About two years ago, I heard God tell me to write but I thought the dream was dead so I did nothing with it. Again, this year I heard "write." I knew God was trying to reawaken that dream! So, thank you, Apostle, for this book and class. This time I won't let the dream die.

Sylvia Sherrod

God has been telling me to write for many years. I would jot things down on any piece of paper I came across. Sometimes I would end up losing or misplacing what I jotted down for the book. But lately, I've had the desire to finish writing the book I started a couple of years ago. This feeling was confirmed when Apostle Tina Beatty announced the class "Let's Write

Together." I truly enjoyed the class from beginning to end and learned the important basics of putting a book together. I realized that writing was something I really enjoyed. I would recommend anyone who has a desire to write to take this class and get the book.

Joy E. Martin
I knew I had a story to tell. But I had no idea how to pull it all together to make sense. This course does that, it teaches you how to pull it all together. The spiritual component to start the process is, what I believe is the key to the success of this class. Fasting and praying for the release of what God wants to say through the writer is very liberating. This class is designed to help the writer overcome fear, writer's block or whatever obstacle that may arise. The writer can go back over the well-explained steps in the e-book or book and start over and continue on with the process of writing your book. Thank you, Apostle Tina Beatty for sharing by example and anointed guidance.

Mattie Morgan
God has blessed me to write ~ now there is no excuse with the 'step-by-step' guide from this class; as well as the opportunity to go back to retrieve information when stuck! Most importantly, however, is having access to a willing instructor who is coaching * pulling * pushing * and beckoning you to FINISH! Thank you, Apostle Beatty.

Let's Write Together

Keisha Freeman
Let's Write Together was both informative and encouraging. The facilitators of the course made it easy and comfortable to write, and understand the process behind getting published. Dr. Beatty's book was a great compliment to the class as well. I would highly recommend this course to anyone looking to start the process of writing. It was certainly a God's sent for me, for such a time as this.

Kathy Clark
As I remember, I just started the class to being held to the ministry, but as I started to write, it brought out a book in me that I really didn't know was there. This class let me know that there is penmanship in me for someone else to read.

Roslyn Williams
Taking the class was very inspirational because when you hear the words: "Write a book;" it seems like it's almost impossible to do. But after taking the class and understanding that there are different types of books that can be written and they don't have to be a novel, it becomes easier to begin because you know that your goal is attainable.

Cornelia Caison
Let's Write Together Webinar blessed me in a whole new way! Even though I'm already an author, there's still a lot that I didn't know. I gained better insight into the do's and don'ts with writing, how to be careful with putting people's names and specific details in your book. This webinar also showed me the kind of writer that I am and also the audience that I'm called to

write to. I wish I had this webinar when I wrote my first book. However, I am glad that I had it while writing my second book and the books to come after!

__Charlene E. Hines__, Founder Of Prayer Fire Ministry
I found the writer's class to be very insightful. It offered quality content to motivate you to initiate your journey as an author. I gained useful information from each speaker, especially about publishing. I would recommend this class as a great writing resource as well as the book which goes along with it.

Let's Write Together

Introduction

Let's Write Together: Write Place, Write Time is a 15-Day writing journey for people who have a desire to write or who have started writing a book but have not completed it. You believe that God has given you a message, a testimony, a strategy, or a word to share with people through your experience and expertise that will bring the reader peace, hope, encouragement, joy, deliverance, healing, or restoration by reading your book.

There may be many reasons why the book or books have not been completed. For example, "I don't have enough time. I start and then I don't like what I wrote so I stop; I keep rewriting what I wrote; I feel as though I don't know what I'm doing; I fear what people will say if they knew my testimony; I feel that I don't have anything to say; What if I fail at writing my book; I get writers block; I get frustrated when I start to write; I don't have any help, or I have a hard time writing."

I find that people often say, "I'm not a writer." However, when you get with likeminded people such as yourself, you will find that you are not alone in the way you think or how you respond to certain situations. There are other people who have the same issues and mental roadblocks when it comes to writing. It becomes a little easier when you surround yourself with people who are also committed to fulfilling their assignments in the earth by releasing the words that have been inspired by God.

Dr. Tina M. Beatty

<u>Habakkuk 2:2</u>
"And the LORD answered me, and said, Write the vision, and make *it* plain upon tables, that he may run that readeth it."

<u>Psalm 45:1</u>
"To the chief Musician upon Shoshannim, for the sons of Korah, Maschil, A Song of loves. My heart is inditing a good matter: I speak of the things which I have made touching the king: my tongue *is* the pen of a ready writer."

<u>Proverbs 27:17</u>
"Iron sharpeneth iron; so a man sharpeneth the countenance of his friend. "

So, with this strategy of having future authors come together for 15 days, the goal is to build self-esteem, encouragement, and endurance as we take this journey together. By working together, each future author will help sharpen the next future author because they are going through this together and wants to see the other succeed. During this time, you will help one another overcome some areas that need to be further developed. It's like what the school system said with the statement, "No Child Left Behind." Well, I say it's "No Future Author Left Behind," either. We also have heard, "Two Are Better Than One." So if two are better than one, then people writing together can strengthen and be supportive and accountable to one another. This all brings togetherness in our writing skills. Writing together brings people together, which produces results!

Let's Write Together

Together means:

- free from emotional or mental agitation.
  Example: She's one of the most *together* people I know.

  Synonyms calm, collected, composed, cool, coolheaded, equal, level, limpid, peaceful, placid, possessed, recollected, sedate, self-composed, self-possessed, serene, smooth, tranquil, undisturbed, unperturbed, unruffled, unshaken, untroubled, unworried (Merriam Webster).

Writing together means you are not alone but someone else is with you and this allows each one to accomplish the same goal by writing and completing a book together.

Dr. Tina M. Beatty

Discovering The Writer In You

Discovering what type of writer you are is very important in becoming an author. This will allow you to become an expert in mastering the subject matter in which you are writing about.

Your discovery will allow you to become more confident in knowing that you have heard instructions from the Lord and you are writing according to His plan for your book.

As we define *discover*, it means to come to an awareness of, to come upon after searching, study or effort, to make known (Merriam Webster Thesaurus). So discovering, in the sense of writing, is to find out the type of writer you are, by being made aware of the hidden potential of the gift, that may have been buried underneath excuses and seeming impossibilities. These treasures are waiting for the appointed time to be discovered by the writer so they can be shared with the world.

Proverbs 3:5-6
Trust in the LORD with all thine heart;
and lean not unto thine own understanding.
In all thy ways acknowledge him,
and he shall direct thy paths.

Luke 1:37
For with God nothing shall be impossible.

Let's Write Together

Discovering the writer in you will help you to pursue the dreams and visions given to you from the Lord, in becoming an author and helping you break free from the fear, that keeps you from writing about your life, past experiences and your testimony. It will also bring breakthrough and deliverance to those who read your book. As you overcome, your readers also overcome and they, in turn, help others to overcome as well. Discovering the writer in you is not just for you but for someone else.

Revelation 12:11
*And they overcame him by the blood of the Lamb,
and by the word of their testimony;
and they loved not their lives unto the death.*

"If you really want to know yourself, start by writing a book."
Shereen El Feki

Discovering the writer in you will remind you of how far you have come and the changes that have taken place within by experiencing God's grace and mercy. This will help you to appreciate what has happened inside you while you are writing from a place of victory.

While you are on this journey, you will be able to pinpoint your particular skills and the area of your specific writing expertise while becoming more comfortable and learning your own unique writing style. What you are most passionate about will begin to surface.

So when you discover what is lodged inside of YOU:

- YOU will write without hesitation
- YOU will write without fear
- YOU will write without shame
- YOU will write without guilt
- YOU will write without doubt
- YOU will write without distractions
- YOU will write with purpose
- YOU will write with determination
- YOU will write until it's complete!

Completion may not be what we think but completion will be according to the timing of the Lord.

Ecclesiastes 3:1
To every thing there is a season,
and a time to every purpose under the heaven:

I share this thought with you because many times, we give ourselves a specific deadline, thinking that we will be finished at that time. However, God may begin to say more to you about what you are writing about or it may simply not be the time to release the book. So we know that timing is key when releasing your book.

Do not become discouraged by the book not being completed by "your" timeline, but keep writing as you are led until it is complete. You may think that time may not be working in your favor, but having a determination to see it through to the end

Let's Write Together

will be your motivation. So keep up the good work and continue to WRITE!

One thing about this 15-day journal is that, if you find that it is taking longer, you can start over and go back to Day 1, and pick up where you left off. It doesn't matter how many times you have to do it, just know that you have this book as a resource that you can look to, to get you back on track.

After you have *discovered* the writer in you, you also want to *acknowledge* the writer in you! Acknowledge means to admit to be real or true; recognize the existence, truth, or fact of; (dictionary.com).

You will *accept* the writer in you! Accept means to take or receive (something offered); receive with approval or favor; (dictionary.com).

You will *encourage* the writer in you! Encourage means to fill with courage or strength of purpose, to help the growth or development of; (Merriam Webster Thesaurus).

You will *believe* in the writer in you! Believe means to consider to be true or honest, to accept the word or evidence of; (Merriam Webster).

You will *commit* to building the writer in you! Commit means to carry through (as a process) to completion; (Merriam Webster Thesaurus).

Dr. Tina M. Beatty

You will *develop* the writer in you! Develop means to gradually become clearer or more detailed, to become mature; (Merriam Webster Thesaurus).

You will *enjoy* the writer in you! Enjoy means to take pleasure in; (Merriam Webster Thesaurus).

You will *love* the writer in you until you can't stop writing! Love means a feeling of strong or constant regard for and dedication to someone; to hold dear, to feel passion, devotion, or tenderness for, to take pleasure in, to touch or handle in a tender or loving manner; (Merriam Webster Thesaurus).

Discovering the writer in you, is altogether rewarding in knowing that something great is on the horizon. In preparation for this journey, I have included blank pages at the back of this book to help begin to draft notes and make sure that you have what you need.

Congratulations on your new book in progress!
Dr. Tina M. Beatty

Let's Write Together

WORD COUNT CHART:

Use this handy table to discover how many pages a given word count yields, single or double spaced, in Times New Roman or Arial 12-point font.

Word Count	Pages (single spaced)	Pages (double spaced)	Font Size
250 WORDS	½ PAGE	1 PAGE	12 POINT
300 WORDS	⅔ PAGE	1⅓ PAGES	12 POINT
400 WORDS	⅘ PAGE	1⅗ PAGES	12 POINT
500 WORDS	1 PAGE	2 PAGES	12 POINT
600 WORDS	1⅓ PAGE	2⅔ PAGES	12 POINT
750 WORDS	1½ PAGES	3 PAGES	12 POINT
800 WORDS	1⅗ PAGES	3⅕ PAGES	12 POINT
1000 WORDS	2 PAGES	4 PAGES	12 POINT
1200 WORDS	2⅖ PAGES	4⅘ PAGES	12 POINT
1500 WORDS	3 PAGES	6 PAGES	12 POINT
2000 WORDS	4 PAGES	8 PAGES	12 POINT
2500 WORDS	5 PAGES	10 PAGES	12 POINT

3000 WORDS	6 PAGES	12 PAGES	12 POINT
3500 WORDS	7 PAGES	14 PAGES	12 POINT
4000 WORDS	8 PAGES	16 PAGES	12 POINT
5000 WORDS	10 PAGES	20 PAGES	12 POINT
6000 WORDS	12 PAGES	24 PAGES	12 POINT
7500 WORDS	15 PAGES	30 PAGES	12 POINT
8000 WORDS	16 PAGES	32 PAGES	12 POINT
10000 WORDS	20 PAGES	40 PAGES	12 POINT

[1]

If you spend approximately one hour writing, you could possibly have written between 800 - 1,000 words. If you are not able to write that many words, the key is that you have made a commitment for one hour which is commendable. Following the standard academic formatting of 12pt. Times New Roman font, and 1" margins, about 350 words can fit on one page.[2]

Do not be too hard on yourself. You are on a journey and you will be proud of the end result, which is finishing your book. Once you get the hang of it, you will be more confident in yourself and trust the content that you are producing.

---

[1] https://wordcounter.io/faq/how-many-pages-is-8000-words/
[2] https://www.answers.com

Let's Write Together

TWELVE WRITING TIPS:

1) People look to you as an expert in your field of interest. What you are saying must be useful, believable and functional. It is time to be passionate about what you are writing about.

2) You must be clear. Your book must have a purpose, which is to inform; to entertain; to encourage; to challenge; to help; to inspire or to give your personal testimony of being an overcomer. Whatever is in your heart to write, write it!

3) Grab the attention of the reader to keep them involved and engaged so they understand or see where you are going with your message. Ultimately you want your reader to be excited and desire to share your future writings with people they know.

4) Read, study and do as much research as you can on the subject or subjects your writing on.

5) Credibility is important when writing. Make sure that the facts that you are presenting are true and you are being honest with your reader. Never take what someone else has written and claim it as your own, that's plagiarism. If you do use someone else's statement or quote, make sure that you have their permission to include it in your writing (blog, articles, book, etc.). Document and always when using a quote or statement from someone else ALWAYS

include the name so they will get the credit and the reader will know where it came from and you won't get in trouble.

6) Can the information you provide in your book be applied to the reader's personal life and be beneficial? Remember if you are writing a book relating to fasting or health issues, you probably will want to include a disclaimer at the beginning of the book.

7) What is it about your book that's different from the other books with this same subject matter?

8) What group of people are you writing too?

9) What you are writing about must be useful based on the person's needs, wants, expectations and desires.

10) One key to being successful is to discover a problem, then through your writing offer the solution to that problem.

11) Write with a purpose and a plan. Know where you are going when writing. Would you be interested in reading the book that you are writing?

12) Write from a place of healing and victory. Not from the place of hurt or pain. If you are not whole in the area that you are writing about your message can put a bad taste in the mouth of your readers. They may not want to buy your books the next time so use wisdom when writing.

Let's Write Together

Proverbs 4:7
"Wisdom *is* the principal thing; *therefore,* get wisdom: and with all thy getting get understanding."

Wisdom is the ability to discern inner qualities and relationships: insight **b:** good sense: judgment **c:** generally accepted belief challenges what has become accepted *wisdom* among many historians — Robert Darnton
d: accumulated philosophical or scientific learning: knowledge
- **2:** a wise attitude, belief, or course of action
- **3:** the teachings of the ancient wise men...
 (Merriam Webster) noun

WRITERS DECREE:

Today, I decree and declare according to Job 22:28, that I will also decree a thing, and it shall be established in my life and the light shall shine upon my ways.

As I begin this 15-Day writing journey, I decree and declare that I will put my trust in the Lord to obey what I hear and begin to write because I know it shall be established to me and the light shall shine upon my ways.

I decree and declare that I will write and complete a book that's been given in my heart to write.

Dr. Tina M. Beatty

I decree and declare that as I write I will be encouraged, empowered, truthful, trustworthy, honest, faithful to my assignment these 15 days.

I decree and declare that I will set aside one hour a day to be in a quiet place with God. I will get away from all distractions, hindrances, noise, people and write consistently what I hear in the spirit, while I am putting pen to paper.

I decree and declare that I will not allow negativity, behaviors, attitudes or thoughts to enter my mind from people or even from myself to interfere with my commitment to write.

I decree and declare that fear, doubt, rejection, and unbelief will not grip my heart or mind. I pronounce judgment upon fear, doubt, rejection, and unbelief and I cancel all assignments sent against me from the enemy, to stop me from writing the book, in Jesus' Name.

I decree and declare that I will surround myself with positive people and other authors who love to write according to God's purpose and plan.

I decree and declare that I will love and enjoy becoming an author, as I encourage myself in the Lord.

I decree and declare that I will WRITE; KEEP WRITING; THEN WRITE SOME MORE until it is finished, Amen!

Let's Write Together

Outline For 15-Day Writing Journey

You need to find a peaceful place where you can quiet your spirit for one hour every day for 15 days, so you write consistently without any interruptions or distractions. Just write what you hear in your spirit, and let it flow. This is why you need a nice, quiet place where you can relax, listen and write.

It's up to you to decide what time of the day you will dedicate your hour; it can be morning, noon, or night. Try not to overthink this time. Allow the peace of God to come over you so you can let it flow.

When you begin writing, make sure that you have everything that you need, such as, paper, pen, pencil, iPad, MacBook, or your computer. The goal is to be prepared so you are not wasting time having to retrieve those items when it's time.

You can write longer than an hour if you desire. The main thing is to be consistent, stay on course, and stick to the plan. Obeying these simple principles will help bring structure into your life as well as break old habits and mindsets that once prevented you from writing and completing your book.

During the first three days, you will pray and seek God for something different every day.

Dr. Tina M. Beatty

DAY 1
Prayer and Fasting Day

Prayer is communicating and fellowshipping with God. During prayer, this is a time where a relationship with the Lord can be established. In prayer, you can talk to the Lord about anything as well as receive answers, revelation, direction, peace, or a specific word. Prayer deepens your relationship by seeking Him daily. Prayer strengthens our heart to believe in Jesus Christ.

According to Strong's Concordance, the word fasting is *tsum*, which means to abstain from food. Essentially, we deny our flesh and abstain from eating food or a type of food (fast as you are led by Holy Spirit).

Listed below are the different types of fasts in the Bible:

One night fast (Daniel 6:18-24)

Three Day fast (Esther 4:16, Acts 9:9)

Seven Day fast (1 Samuel 31:13, 2 Samuel 12:16-23)

Fourteen Day fast (Acts 27:33-34)

Twenty-one Day fast (Daniel 10:3-13)

Forty Day fast (Deuteronomy 9:9, 1 Kings 19:8, Matthew 4:2)

Let's Write Together

Matthew 17:21
"Howbeit this kind goeth not out but by prayer and fasting."

Isaiah 58:6-8
6 Is not this the fast that I have chosen? to loose the bands of wickedness, to undo the heavy burdens, and to let the oppressed go free, and that ye break every yoke?

7 Is it not to deal thy bread to the hungry, and that thou bring the poor that are cast out to thy house? when thou seest the naked, that thou cover him; and that thou hide not thyself from thine own flesh?

8 Then shall thy light break forth as the morning, and thine health shall spring forth speedily: and thy righteousness shall go before thee; the glory of the Lord shall be thy reward.

Note: Whatever is revealed during your time of prayer and fasting. Write it down, find scriptures to meditate on that will help you break free.

Joshua 1:8-9
8 This book of the law shall not depart out of thy mouth; but thou shalt meditate therein day and night, that thou mayest observe to do according to all that is written therein: for then thou shalt make thy way prosperous, and then thou shalt have good success.
9 Have not I commanded thee? Be strong and of a good courage; be not afraid, neither be thou dismayed: for the Lord thy God is with thee whithersoever thou goest.

Day 2
Prayer and Fasting from the Spirit of Fear

Fear is to experience concern or anxiety; Her friends *feared* that she was dating a guy who was all wrong for her
Synonyms bother, fret, fuss, stew, stress, sweat, trouble, worry verb (Merriam Webster Thesaurus)

The Spirit of Fear has torment and can paralyze people from writing to prevent them from moving forward. Fear will keep you from succeeding in anything you have set your heart to do.

<u>2 Timothy 1:7</u>
"For God hath not given us the spirit of fear; but of power, and of love, and of a sound mind."

<u>Deuteronomy 31:6</u>
"Be strong and of a good courage, fear not, nor be afraid of them: for the Lord thy God, he *it is* that doth go with thee; he will not fail thee, nor forsake thee."

<u>1 John 4:18</u>
"There is no fear in love; but perfect love casteth out fear: because fear hath torment. He that feareth is not made perfect in love."

Note: Whatever is revealed to you during your time of prayer and fasting time be sure that you write it down.

Let's Write Together

Day 3
Pray to receive the vision, title, subjects, outline, research and study tools

Habakkuk 2:2
And the Lord answered me, and said, Write the vision, and make *it* plain upon tables, that he may run that readeth it.

Jeremiah 29:11
"For I know the thoughts that I think toward you, saith the Lord, thoughts of peace, and not of evil, to give you an expected end."

Matthew 5:8
"Blessed *are* the pure in heart: for they shall see God."

Day 4
First Day of Your Writing Journey

Psalm 37:5-6
⁵ Commit thy way unto the LORD; trust also in him; and he shall bring it to pass.

⁶ And he shall bring forth thy righteousness as the light, and thy judgment as the noonday

Quotes on Commitment:
"There's a difference between interest and commitment. When you're interested in doing something, you do it only when

circumstance permit. When you're committed to something, you accept no excuses, only results." – Art Turock

Stay committed to your decisions but stay flexible in your approach." – Tony Robbins

Day 5
Second Day of Your Writing Journey

Deuteronomy 31:6
"Be strong and of a good courage, fear not, nor be afraid of them: for the LORD thy God, he *it is* that doth go with thee; he will not fail thee, nor forsake thee."

Quotes on Courage:
"Success is not final, failure is not fatal: it is the courage to continue that counts." Winston Churchill

"I learned that courage was not the absence of fear but the triumph over it." Nelson Mandela

Day 6
Third Day of Your Writing Journey

John 7:38
"He that believeth on me, as the scripture hath said, out of his belly shall flow rivers of living water."

Let's Write Together

Quotes on Flow:
"Surrender to the flow."- Mike Gordon

"Being in the flow means being aware that the river of life is flowing to us at every moment. Being in the flow means accepting whatever comes and putting it to good use, before passing it on. Going with the flow means allowing whatever comes to move on freely, without holding on in any way." - Anonymous

Day 7
Fourth Day of Your Writing Journey

<u>Hebrews 11:1</u>
"Now faith is the substance of things hoped for, the evidence of things not seen."

Quotes on Faith:
"Faith is taking the first step even when you don't see the whole staircase. – Martin Luther King, Jr.

Feed your faith and your fear will starve." – Anonymous

Day 8
Fifth Day of Your Writing Journey

<u>Proverbs 16:3</u>
"Commit thy works unto the LORD, and thy thoughts shall be established. "

Quotes on Focus:
"Focus is the key to accomplish what is necessary - easy word to spell, it contains only five letters but it is probably one of the most powerful words there are in order to move forward with confidence and with the expected results." - Byron Pulsifer,

"As soon as you focus, things will start coming together... Once I focused on this one opportunity... big things started happening." - Brandon Webb

Day 9
Sixth Day of Your Writing Journey

<u>*Colossians 1:11*</u>
"Strengthened with all might, according to his glorious power, unto all patience and longsuffering with joyfulness;

Quote on Endurance:
"Nothing great is ever achieved without much enduring
-Anonymous

"There are no shortcuts to endurance. You have to train yourself to make peace with the long route, every day, and do it, and love where it is taking you." - Anonymous

Let's Write Together

Day 10
Seventh Day of Your Writing Journey

Philippians 4:7-9

7 And the peace of God, which passeth all understanding, shall keep your hearts and minds through Christ Jesus.

8 Finally, brethren, whatsoever things are true, whatsoever things are honest, whatsoever things are just, whatsoever things are pure, whatsoever things are lovely, whatsoever things are of good report; if there be any virtue, and if there be any praise, think on these things.

9 Those things, which ye have both learned, and received, and heard, and seen in me, do: and the God of peace shall be with you.

Quotes on Peace: "Peace is not merely a distant goal that we seek, but a means by which we arrive at that goal."
- Martin Luther King Jr."

"Peace is costly but it is worth the expense." – African Proverb

Day 11
Eighth Day of Your Writing Journey

Psalm 100:1-5
A Psalm of praise. Make a joyful noise unto the Lord, all ye lands.

2 Serve the Lord with gladness: come before his presence with singing.

3 Know ye that the Lord he is God: it is he that hath made us, and not we ourselves; we are his people, and the sheep of his pasture.

4 Enter into his gates with thanksgiving, and into his courts with praise: be thankful unto him, and bless his name.

5 For the Lord is good; his mercy is everlasting, and his truth endureth to all generations.

Quote on Praise: "When you focus on how wonderful God is and all the great things He's done... is doing... and even will do in your life, your natural response will be praise, adoration, and awe. Don't let yourself ever get used to it... stay amazed!"
- Joyce Meyer

"All our actions, as well as our thoughts and words, should praise Him who always blesses us." - Charles Spurgeon

Day 12
Introduction, Foreword, Table of Contents, Chapters, Preface

Introduction - written by the author and deals with the subject of the book, supplementing and introducing the concept or indicating a point of view for the reader when being read.

Let's Write Together

Foreword - a short introductory statement in a published work, as a book, especially when written by someone other than the author.[3] Someone who is an expert in the topic or field if possible. A foreword by a well-known or respected individual lends credibility to your work.

Table of Contents - usually headed simply contents and abbreviated informally as TOC, is a list, usually found on a page before the start of a written work, of its chapter or section titles or brief descriptions with their commencing page numbers.[4] The table of contents has the layout of the chapters and chronological order in which it should flow to help the reader know what is expected when reading the book.

Chapters - is the main division of a piece of writing of relative length, such as a book of prose, poetry, or law. A chapter book may have multiple chapters and these can be referred to by the things that may be the main topic of that specific chapter. In each case, chapters can be numbered or titled or both.[5]

Preface - is a preliminary statement in a book by the author or editor, setting forth its purpose and scope, expressing acknowledgment of assistance from others, etc.[6]

---

[3] https://www.dictionary.com/browse/foreword
[4] https://en.wikipedia.org/wiki/Table_of_contents
[5] https://en.wikipedia.org/wiki/Chapter
[6] https://www.dictionary.com/browse/preface

Day 13
Appendix, Biography, Acknowledgments & Photo

Appendix - when you include any closing materials such as endnotes, glossary, study guides, articles, document, other text, about the author, etc.

Biography - usually written history of a person's life. (Merriam-Webster).

Write a short bio introducing yourself. This should include what you want the reader to know about yourself, do you a favorite saying, a favorite scripture, a favorite quote, a testimony, what makes you unique and what makes you an expert on this subject matter?

Use only the most pertinent details as they relate to demonstrating your expertise for the book your writing, create a list of your notable achievements, accomplishments, leadership positions, organizations, businesses, education, credentials, awards, other books you have written, family status such as to whom you are married and how long, your children and grandchildren (if appropriate), name your degrees and add a closing statement.

You may not use all of this but it's always best to be prepared for the specific bio you must provide for each book you write.

Let's Write Together

Acknowledgments are made up of expressions of gratitude, appreciation, something or someone valuable, indebtedness to others, etc.

You will need a professional photo taken for your book. I cannot stress enough how important it is to have a professional photographer to take your picture. Also, you will need to have a professional makeup artist do your makeup for your photoshoot. You have come too far to use a "selfie" you took from your cellphone to be used on this important work. Make the proper investment. If you need to wait until you have the funds to make it happen, you will not regret it.

Day 14
Catch Up and Review Day

Day 15
Completion Day

Dr. Tina M. Beatty

10 Launching Tips To Prepare You

1. Identify your book's targeted audience. Many authors make the mistake of thinking everyone is going to read their book, but in reality, some people are more likely to purchase their book than others. As a writer, you should answer the question: Does your writing appeal more to women, men, young adults, teenagers, youth or children? Or is it for leadership, entrepreneurs, business owners, church, ministry, family, marriage, parenting, singles, cooking, education, life coaching, addictions, deliverance, healing, restoration or whatever the Lord has put upon your heart to write about? This will help you to narrow down the type of audience you will be writing to, so you won't be all over the place, but be right where the Lord would have you to be, for that particular book.

2. Create a marketing plan and promote your book locally, then gradually expand by creating flyers, advertising, radio, newspaper, television, business cards, posters, email blast, text blast, letters, whatever way to get the word out, do it because this will get the attention of your audience. When you start locally, where you live, you open the door for the people to receive you before you begin to reach out to other cities and nations. You make sure you value the place where you live, to gain the respect of who you are as a writer. How much time will you devote to establishing and maintaining your book promotion strategies?

Let's Write Together

3.   Create a great elevator pitch about your book. It should be at least 2 or 3 sentences of a brief focused message aimed toward a particular person or group that summarizes why they should purchase your book. This is a good way of catching the attention of the people that this book is written for.

4.   Network by telling your family and friends about your book because this will strengthen your support system and they can share in the excitement with you, for the release of your book. This will prepare you to expand your reach when it's time, to your coworkers, business partners, church members, organizations, networks, book clubs, social media friends or people connected to you.

5.   Establish a budget. This way you will not overspend, you will know exactly how much money is to be spent on marketing and promoting your book. This will help you to be a good steward of the budget that you have set for yourself. Don't forget to include all travel expenses when promoting your book.

6.   Build an email list and direct the people to your website to subscribe and get more information concerning your book. Make visiting your website worthwhile by providing remarkable content. Use the list to create and build a buzz for the launch of your book. Try to keep the people interested in the book, by asking for feedback so they will become invested in the successful outcome of your book. And this way you can make necessary changes if needed and receive testimonials that you can add to your website or blogs, which will help you in becoming a credible writer. With every email sent out be sure to

include information on the new upcoming book, events, announcements, projects, speaking engagements or anything else that will be productive to your success as an author.

7. How will they purchase your book? Email, Christian Bookstores, Bookstores, Website, Amazon, Barnes and Nobles, Kindle, Books A Million, etc., and will your book be in English only or other translation as well, when purchasing the book? Will you have an e-book, workbook, manual, devotional or journal to go along with your book? Will it be hardback or a paperback book?

8. Take Advantage of Social Media, you can build a platform for your book to be launched such as Twitter, YouTube, Facebook, Instagram, LinkedIn, Pinterest, Periscope, etc., plus it will give you free advertisement.

9. Advertise your previous books in each book you publish, because this will excite the reader and they will have an expectancy of the release of your next upcoming books.

10. Develop a webinar or workshop based on the content or chapters of your book. This will draw attention to those the book was written for as well as generate an audience for potential readers.

Let's Write Together

About the Author

Apostle Tina M. Beatty is the Founder and Senior Pastor of King of Glory International Ministries and Lion of Judah International Ministries in Charleston, West Virginia. She received her Doctorate of Divinity from St. Thomas Christian University.

She is anointed to teach and preach deliverance to the captives with power and authority throughout the United States as well as Internationally. Apostle Beatty is a wife and mother of four children and five grandchildren.

She has ministered as well as led conferences such as, PrayerQuake and *I Lived To Tell It Deliverance and Healing Conference* (which was birthed through her personal deliverance and healing), retreats, revivals, churches, workshops, and I Lived To Tell It Bootcamp, "Diamond in the Rough." She is not ashamed to tell her testimony and let the people know that whatever you have done or whatever was done to you, YOU CAN LIVE and LIVE TO TELL IT!

Revelation 12:11
And they overcame him by the Blood of the Lamb and by the word of their testimony; and they loved not their lives unto the death.

She is also an entrepreneur with many businesses: Nappy by Nature Salon, Strategic Life Coach Academy, The Apostle's Closet, TMBeatty Ministries Inc., King of Glory Apostolic Network, King of Glory Worldwide Ministries, Kingdom

Dr. Tina M. Beatty

Leadership Academy, King of Glory Unlimited Travel and I Lived to Tell It, LLC. Contributing Author of *Breathe Again* (Author of the Chapter, Forgive Again).

Let's Write Together

Dr. Tina M. Beatty

Let's Write Together

Dr. Tina M. Beatty

Let's Write Together

Dr. Tina M. Beatty

Let's Write Together

Dr. Tina M. Beatty

Let's Write Together

Dr. Tina M. Beatty

Let's Write Together

Dr. Tina M. Beatty

Let's Write Together

Dr. Tina M. Beatty

Let's Write Together

Dr. Tina M. Beatty

Let's Write Together

Dr. Tina M. Beatty

Let's Write Together

Dr. Tina M. Beatty

Let's Write Together

Dr. Tina M. Beatty

Let's Write Together

Dr. Tina M. Beatty

Let's Write Together

Dr. Tina M. Beatty

Let's Write Together

Dr. Tina M. Beatty

Let's Write Together

Dr. Tina M. Beatty

Let's Write Together

Dr. Tina M. Beatty

Let's Write Together

Dr. Tina M. Beatty

Let's Write Together

Dr. Tina M. Beatty

Let's Write Together

Dr. Tina M. Beatty

Let's Write Together

Dr. Tina M. Beatty

Let's Write Together

Dr. Tina M. Beatty

Let's Write Together

Dr. Tina M. Beatty

Let's Write Together

Dr. Tina M. Beatty

Let's Write Together

Dr. Tina M. Beatty

Let's Write Together

Dr. Tina M. Beatty

Let's Write Together

Dr. Tina M. Beatty

Let's Write Together

Dr. Tina M. Beatty

Let's Write Together

Dr. Tina M. Beatty

Let's Write Together

Dr. Tina M. Beatty

Let's Write Together

Dr. Tina M. Beatty

Let's Write Together

Dr. Tina M. Beatty

Let's Write Together

Dr. Tina M. Beatty

Let's Write Together

Dr. Tina M. Beatty

www.ingramcontent.com/pod-product-compliance
Lightning Source LLC
LaVergne TN
LVHW061345060426
835512LV00012B/2578